# HOW TO OVERCOME LONELINESS

by Elisabeth Elliot

A MINISTRY OF THE NAVIGATORS
P.O. BOX 6000, COLORADO SPRINGS, COLORADO 80934

The Navigators is an international Christian organization. Jesus Christ gave His followers the Great Commission to go and make disciples (Matthew 28:19). The aim of The Navigators is to help fulfill that commission by multiplying laborers for Christ in every nation.

NavPress is the publishing ministry of The Navigators. NavPress publications are tools to help Christians grow. Although publications alone cannot make disciples or change lives, they can help believers learn biblical discipleship, and apply what they learn to their lives and ministries.


ISBN 08910-95748

**The content of this booklet is adapted from *Loneliness* by Elisabeth Elliot, published by Oliver-Nelson Books. To fully benefit from the author's message, the reader is encouraged to enjoy a complete reading of *Loneliness*, which is available through Christian bookstores.**



Printed in the United States of America

# HOW TO OVERCOME LONELINESS

*At midnight in a silent airplane, a man reaches to light his companion's cigarette. I can see the outline of his hand, the knuckles and fingers, the hairs illuminated for a few seconds. The woman draws, puffs a thin column of smoke. A click. Darkness.*

*Only the most ordinary of gestures, meaning almost nothing to them. But for me, sitting by the window looking out again at the cold stars, it speaks of a whole world that is lost to me now. A man and a woman. Together. His hand stretched toward her to help.*

*I am traveling alone, a widow. I remember another hand—a bit bigger than that one with fingers strong for wrestling and carpentry, dexterous for drawing, tender for caressing. I can still see the square fingernails, and how the hair grew on the back of that hand. The man it belonged to has been gone more than a year, long enough for me to have difficulty remembering how it felt when he touched me, how it was to put my hand inside his.*

*I lean my forehead against the glass and a great heaving tide pours over me, drowns me—as it has done a hundred times in the past year. But there are so many so much worse off than I. I remember that. How blessed I have been, to have been a wife even for a short time. Yet, in the most unpremeditated ways, in the oddest places and for the most absurd reasons—as I'm going about my business, generally calm, even cheerful—that sudden tide sweeps in. It's called loneliness.*

## From Alone to Lonely

God created man and woman to be partners. Each, however, was still profoundly alone—in a separate body, alone before God, bearing His image, answering to Him, responsible. This aloneness was a good thing, for everything in the garden was perfect.

But sin destroyed that perfect harmony. The relationship of man with God and other humans was fractured. Man now *knows* that he is alone. His aloneness is no longer an experience only of solitude (not by any means a bad thing in itself) but also of deprivation. The human companionship, which in the divine plan was the answer to man's aloneness, no longer suffices. Man's aloneness has gained a dimension of pain—a pain called loneliness.

The world's poor anodynes are eagerly

seized—"I *might* find the answer in the singles' bar, the personal column, the dating service." Truly the lonely might find a mate, someone willing to have a go at loving them, at least for a night, but is this really the answer they seek? Without a foothold, without an awareness of being a part of something grander and greater than themselves, it will not be enough.

For me, the answer to loneliness is not to solve or assuage it, but to embrace it as a gift from a loving Father and to offer it back to Him, so that He can transform it into a gift for others.

## Fierceness and Tenderness

The love of God brought us all into being—sun, stars, winds, men and women, and "infants to sweeten the world." To know God, or even to begin to know Him, is to know that we are not alone in the universe. *Someone Else is out there.* There is a hint that there may be a refuge for our loneliness. To stop our frantic getting, spending, and searching, and simply to *look* at the things God has made is to move one step away from despair. For God cares. The most awesome seascape can reveal a care that is actually *tender*.

"Who watched over the birth of the sea, when it burst in flood from the womb?" God asked Job in the midst of his great suffering, "when I wrapped it in a blanket of cloud and cradled it in fog" (Job 38:8-9). A God who can look on the mighty ocean as a tiny newborn—could He overlook one of His lonely people? Job had felt very much overlooked. Yet, after all his questions and accusations, he was shown that not for a moment had he really been forgotten.

"Do you . . . attend the wild doe when she is in labour? Do you count the months that they carry their young or know the time of their delivery, when they crouch down to open their wombs . . . ?" (Job 39:1-3). If God attends the doe in the throes of her agony, we may believe that an aching heart does not escape His notice.

My parents taught their children in a thousand ways to know the One who made us all, and to trust Him. And they told us the story that, far more than all the glories of nature, opens the heart of God—the story of the One "who is the effulgence of God's splendour and the stamp of God's very being" (Hebrews 1:3)—the story of Jesus; His birth, His life, His death on the cross. When we were very small they taught us to trust Him; they sang to us at bedtime, "Safe in the arms of Jesus."

But safety, as the Cross shows, does not exclude suffering. As I began to grow up and learn about suffering, I learned that *trust* in those strong arms means that even our suffering is under control. We are not doomed to meaninglessness. A loving purpose is behind it all, a great tenderness even in the fierceness.

Knowing that my aloneness comes from the hand of a loving Father enables me to receive it as a gift, not a curse. Among the many letters I received after Jim's death, one came from a college classmate of his, telling me how her husband (a missionary) had walked into the kitchen one day with the grocery bags, banged them down on the counter, said, "I'm leaving you," turned on his heel, and walked out the door. She wanted me to be aware that there are much worse ways of losing a husband than death. I have never had any doubt about that.

Bonnie, another divorced friend, sent me a card on which were printed the words of Psalm 68:6 (NASB): "God makes a home for the lonely." Her letter said,

> I was reading the Psalms one night when I really saw that verse for the first time. I was still making the adjustment to coming home to an empty apartment at night and I was more scared than I wanted to admit. . . . There were no notes waiting when I opened the door, no signs of life, and worst of all, no one expecting me. The reality was beginning to sink in: despite friends and family who cared about me, I was essentially *alone* for the first time in my life.
>
> So I was surprised—even shocked—to see my situation right there

in print. *God makes a home for the lonely*. How? It seemed to me to be a rather bold statement. Yet I knew from experience that God does not make empty promises.

When we think of being lonely, we usually mean that there are no people around; no one with us, no one to talk to. Or else we find that the people around us are "not on our wavelength"—they don't understand us, and that can be worse than no company at all. So loneliness in my experience is not relieved by just anyone's company. It needs to be someone special—someone who understands me, someone who can listen and *be there when I need them*. It was this last part that forced me to confront the depth of my own loneliness. Of all my friends, no one person could be with me all the time. And even if they could, none of them had the power to do anything about my situation. It was ultimately my problem.

Yet here was the Bible saying that God could do something about my loneliness. As a matter of fact, if you look at the rest of the psalm, is says that God can "do something" about a lot of things. Nothing is too hard for Him. The psalmist goes on to elaborate from history exactly what that means: God is always on the side of His people in their battle for survival; from the massive exodus from Egypt to the individual plight of widows and orphans. He cares about justice. He is full of mercy. The giant scope of His power in world affairs does not cause Him to overlook our individual concerns. And He has come to earth to prove it. Because of that, He can sympathize with our weakness. He understands our feelings because being human, He has experienced loneliness too.

Here's a Person who not only understands me but who fascinates me—a Person whom I have become thrilled to know. Christ calls me out of my natural self-centeredness by listening to my cries and then showing me the bigger picture. The better I come to know Him, the more I become interested in what He is interested in—the more I live and breathe for His Kingdom to come, for things to be done on earth as they are in Heaven.

As the time of year approaches when we begin talking about going home for the holidays, these things become even more real to me. Where is my home ultimately? My home is where Christ is. My apartment has become a home because I share it with Him. As I have worked to make it a comfortable place to be, I have discovered new ways of expressing the gift of hospitality that He has nurtured in me through the years. God has made a home for me in order for me to share that home with others.

"God makes a home for the lonely" can also be translated "God sets the lonely in families." Through the last year I have come to know the reality of a much bigger family than my own natural family, dear as they are to me. My larger family are those who also know Christ in an intimate way. They are the ones who have listened to my cries and at the same time encouraged me to consider issues larger than myself. They are the ones whom God has used not only to relieve my loneliness, but to deepen my love for the Kingdom. As I find my place of service within the community of God's people, there is little time left to feel lonely!

My joy is becoming less dependent upon my own immediate circumstances and more attached to what God is doing. As limited as my understanding is now, I know that He is a God who never loses, a God who has taken the ultimate humiliation and defeat and turned it inside out. Somehow my ruined plans fit into His larger plans. And so in the moments when I am forced to face my own loneliness, I find that I am not really alone at all!

Bonnie and I have been reading the same Book, have found its truth transforming. God is in the business of "turning things inside out."

Her letter illustrates what I call the *gift* of loneliness. Bonnie's has become not only a gift for her (look at the spiritual gains), but like all God's gifts, a gift for the rest of us—the people who share her hospitality, for example, and the people whom she is now able to console, including you and me. She testifies that she no longer has much time to brood about it.

If God had eliminated the problem, He would have eliminated the particular kind of blessing that it bears. If Bonnie had not taken her troubles in the right spirit, she would have missed that blessing. By acceptance, she was laying her will alongside His, willing to cooperate, willing to put herself in the yoke with Him. Now she is actually finding that His yoke, so burdensome if borne all alone, is light. She has found that acceptance brings peace.

## Make Me a Cake

Loneliness is something not only to be accepted but something also to be offered, as the body God gives each of us is meant to be an offering. Give it back.

> With eyes wide open to the mercies of God, I beg you . . . as an act of intelli-

gent worship, to give him your bodies, as a living sacrifice, consecrated to him and acceptable by him. (Romans 12:1, PH)

The love of God in accepting such an offering is like the love of a father whose little child gives him a present bought with money the father gave him. It is a very tender, sympathetic love. It recognizes that the child's loving gift comes out of his utter poverty. The father, who has already given everything, gives something more in order that his child may have something to give.

What may we give? Everything—everything God has given us—time, work, prayers, possessions, praise, and yes, sufferings. In this mysterious sense, loneliness is a gift not only to be received, but one to be offered as a holy sacrifice.

Some people see singleness as a liability, a deprivation, even a curse. Others see it as a huge asset, a license to be a "swinger," an opportunity to do what feels good. I see it as a gift. To make that gift an offering may be the most costly thing one can do, for it means laying down a cherished dream of what one wanted to be, and accepting what one did not want to be.

During the months of my second husband's terminal illness I sometimes felt I could not bear one more day of seeing him suffer, or one more visit to the doctor who would tell us terrible things that must be done next—

things like removing the lower jaw because of the lip cancer, or castration because of the prostate cancer. Everything in me said, *No no no no*. Add's suffering became mine. The wee hours were filled with nightmarish images of things far worse than death, and I was afraid. What to do?

The answer came to me.

"Offer it up."

My eyes had been opened to this possibility through the reading of Evelyn Underhill's classic, *The Mystery of Sacrifice*. I had never before been taught the deep truth of making all of life an oblation, but this little book had come into my hands just three months before we discovered my husband's illness. I do not know what I would have done without it.

Offer up *what?* I felt like the destitute widow of Zarephath, about to use the last of the flour and oil, which stood between her sons' and her own starvation, when along came Elijah who told her to bake him a cake first. Because it was the word of the Lord, she obeyed. The effects of that obedience went far beyond her imagination. "There was food for him and for her and her family for a long time. The jar of flour did not give out nor did the flask of oil fail, as the word of the LORD foretold through Elijah" (1 Kings 17:15-16).

I had nothing in the house. Nothing except this pain. Pain—an offering? What could the Lord possibly make of that?

"Make me a cake." In other words, Elijah

said: There is one thing you can do. Even from your poverty, you can give me something. It may not seem like much, but it is the very thing I need. If you will give it to me I can do something I could not do without it.

"The sacrifices of God are a broken spirit: a broken and a contrite heart, O God, thou wilt not despise" (Psalm 51:17, KJV).

So, as best I could, I offered it up.

That was fifteen years ago. It has taken me a long time to assimilate this great lesson. I have not yet mastered it. But my understanding of sacrifice has been transformed. It has also transformed my life. The emphasis now is not on loss, privation, or a price to be paid. I see it as an act of intelligent worship, and as a gift God has given me to give back to Him *in order that He may make something of it.*

When Add died in September of 1973, the Lord in His mercy helped me to see a little more clearly in my second widowhood what I had only dimly descried in the first: a gift, a call, and a vocation, not merely a condition to be endured. Paul's words came alive: "Each one must order his life according to the gift the Lord has granted him" (1 Corinthians 7:17).

So it was the Lord who had put into my hands this gift of widowhood. *Is this the little "cake" You need from me, Lord? Then I'll bake it for You, Lord. Please have it.*

And what next? "I will offer . . . the sacrifice of thanksgiving" (Psalm 116:17, NKJV). It is wonderfully comforting to be absolutely sure that we do the will of God. Here is one matter about which there can be no doubt: "Be thankful, whatever the circumstances may be. For this is the will of God for you in Christ Jesus" (1 Thessalonians 5:18, PH).

## The King and the Beggar

Can we give up all for the love of God? When the surrender of ourselves seems too much to ask, it is first of all because our thoughts about God Himself are paltry. We have not really seen Him, we have hardly tested Him at all and learned how good He is. In our blindness we approach Him with suspicious reserve. We ask how much of our fun He intends to spoil, how much He will demand from us, how high is the price we must pay before He is placated. If we had the least notion of His lovingkindness and tender mercy, His Fatherly care for His poor children, His generosity, His beautiful plans for us; if we knew how patiently He waits for our turning to Him, how gently He means to lead us to green pastures and still waters, how carefully He is preparing a place for us, how ceaselessly He is ordering and ordaining and engineering His master plan for our good—if we had any inkling of all this, could we be reluctant to let go of our smashed dandelions or whatever we clutch so fiercely in our sweaty little hands?

If with courage and joy we pour ourselves out for Him and for others for His sake, it is not possible to lose, in any final sense, anything worth keeping. We will lose ourselves and our selfishness. We will gain everything worth having. But what if we hold back?

There is an old story of a king who went into the village streets to greet his subjects. A beggar sitting by the roadside eagerly held up his almsbowl, sure that the king would give handsomely. Instead, the king asked the beggar to give him something. Taken aback, the beggar fished three grains of rice from his bowl and dropped them into the king's outstretched hand. When at the end of the day the beggar poured out what he had received, he found to his astonishment three grains of pure gold in the bottom of his bowl. *O that I had given him all!*

## No Agenda of My Own

What will God do with this cake offered back? He will enable us to turn loneliness into solitude and solitude into prayer—into beauty for us, for others, for Himself.

It takes the fire of God to cleanse our hearts of subtle selfishness. Even loneliness may be a form of selfishness. One can reject friendship when it is not offered on the terms one chooses. One can magnify his loneliness out of all proportion, as though he suffered something that is not common to man, forgetting that "this is life"—not more, not less. One can draw about himself a thick quilt of self-pity and isolate himself in other ways. But if one turns the loneliness into solitude and the solitude into prayer, there is release. It may require a willingness to be burned if burning is necessary, but there is forgiveness and cleansing and peace.

For the prophet Isaiah, standing alone before God meant nakedness, burning, and then a call for a volunteer to work for God. With a heart now burnt free from itself, Isaiah could answer, "Here I am; send me" (Isaiah 6; see verses 1-7). In this way, Isaiah turned his solitude into prayer.

I was pondering this matter when the Lord brought to my kitchen table a living example of such a heart. A bright young woman and I were eating lamb sandwiches. I asked her if she is lonely.

"Lonely? Why should I be?"

"You're single. Most of the single people I know talk about being lonely."

With a look of surprise and then a laugh she said, "Oh, no. You see, I have a sense of expectancy every day. What does the Lord want to do with me today? I have no agenda of my own."

*No agenda of my own*. There is the key to Linda's freedom. I continued to question her. Yes, she said, she knows what loneliness feels like—it's isolation, when you think you can't reach anybody, nobody reaches you, you're cut off. You have your own agenda.

"What do you mean by agenda?" I asked.

"Thinking there's only one solution, and God has to give you that or nothing. You have a closed mind. A closed mind is a closed heart and a closed door."

Now I recognized the reason for the smile that seems always to light Linda's face. It comes from her wholehearted acceptance of *God's* "agenda."

"I love solitude," she said. "As I drove up here this morning [it was a dazzling winter morning of sunshine and blue sky and blue shadows on the snow] I didn't have the radio on. I wasn't listening to tapes. I was just quiet. I love times like that."

The heart with no agenda but God's is the heart at leisure from itself. Its emptiness is filled with the love of God. Its solitude can be turned into prayer.

## A Gate of Hope

I met Katherine Morgan in New York City in 1952, when she had brought her four daughters from Colombia for high school. She worked for a missionary magazine called *Voices*, in a tiny office in a dismal building near City Hall. I sometimes helped her there, doing odd jobs for the staff.

We usually ate lunch in the office, making tea in a seedy little washroom and sometimes feasting on cold mutton pies brought in by the editor, a Scot. I plied Katherine with questions about her life as missionary, wife, mother, widow. She answered them always with good humor and often downright hilarity. When I probed things most of us would call problems, she made light of them.

One day, in answer to a question, she said, "I'm sure I'm a better woman because I'm a widow than I would have been otherwise."

She was unfailingly thoughtful and kind to the old man she worked under; she took time for me, a hopeful missionary candidate; she has laid down her life daily for more than half a century in Pasto and now in Bogota. She has kept open house for anybody and everybody—the poor, the sorrowing, the ill, the insane, the outcasts, the criminals, and the dying. Anyone who needs a mother and a home and love finds them all at Katherine's. She does it not merely unselfishly; she does it with no thought of self whatsoever.

> Blessed are [those] whose strength is
> in thee,
> in whose heart are the highways
> to Zion.
> As they go through the valley of Baca
> they make it a place of springs. . . .
> They go from strength to strength.
> (Psalm 84:5-7, RSV)

Katherine's valley of Baca (weeping) has been made a place of springs for me and for thousands of Colombians. For me she stands as irrefutable proof that the answer to our loneliness is *love*—not our finding someone to love us, but our surrendering to the God who has always loved us with an everlasting love. Loving Him is then expressed in a joyful and full-hearted pouring out of ourselves in love to others.

I'm a long way behind Katherine and all the rest who have so brightly shown me this pathway to God. But I have His promise: "I will woo her, I will go with her into the wilderness and comfort her: there I will restore her vineyards, turning the Vale of Trouble into the Gate of Hope" (Hosea 2:14-15).

**Summary**

Loneliness is one of the terms of our humanness and so, in a sense, incurable. Yet in the wilderness of loneliness, God wants to give us Himself. I have found peace in my loneliest times not only through *accepting* the situation as my loving Father's gift to me, but through *offering* it back to Him, who can transfigure it: wilderness into watered garden, my little death into life for others. The key is surrendering myself and my agenda to Him and His, embracing His fierce and tender love.

## For Reflection and Action

1. Describe your feelings of loneliness on paper, to another person, or aloud to God. Tell Him exactly how you feel.

2. a. How have you tried to handle your feelings up to now?

   b. What have been the results?

3. a. How has God made a home for Bonnie, Linda, and Katherine in their loneliness?

   b. How has loneliness proven to be a gift for each of them?

   c. Ask God for the strength and courage to receive your loneliness as a gift and to offer it back to Him.

4. Stand, sit, or kneel before God with your palms held open upward as though you were receiving or offering something. Be silent for a few minutes, putting yourself consciously in His presence. Think of Him. Then think of what you have received from Him—what you are, what you have, what you do, what you suffer. Thank the Lord for whatever aspect of this gift you can honestly thank Him for—if not for the gift itself, then for its transformability, His will that allows you to have this gift, His presence in the midst of it. Then offer it back. Lift your hands as a physical sign of your love, acceptance, and trust.

   Don't look for dramatic effects. Let God's answer appear in His time and way.

## For Meditation

Read one of the following passages several times a day, and think about what it means for your life:

*God makes a home for the lonely;*
*He leads out the prisoners into*
*prosperity,*
*Only the rebellious dwell in a parched*
*land.* (Psalm 68:6, NASB)

*A father to the fatherless, a defender*
*of widows,*
*is God in his holy dwelling.*
*God sets the lonely in families,*
*he leads forth the prisoners with*
*singing.* (Psalm 68:5-6, NIV)

*Blessed are [those] whose strength is*
*in thee,*
*in whose heart are the highways*
*to Zion.*
*As they go through the valley of Baca*
*[weeping]*
*they make it a place of springs. . . .*
*They go from strength to strength.*
(Psalm 84:5-7, RSV)

**The *NavPress Booklet Series* includes:**

**God Cares About Your Work**
by Doug Sherman & William Hendricks

**Building Your Child's Self-Esteem**
by Gary Smalley & John Trent

**How to Have a Quiet Time**
by Warren & Ruth Myers

**When You Disagree: Resolving Marital Conflicts**
by Jack & Carole Mayhall

**Your Words Can Make a Difference**
by Carole Mayhall

**You Can Trust God**
by Jerry Bridges

**How to Know God's Will**
by Charles Stanley

**How to Overcome Loneliness**
by Elisabeth Elliot

**How to Keep Your Head Up When Your Job's Got You Down**
by Doug Sherman

**How to Deal with Anger**
by Dr. Larry Crabb

**How to Handle Stress**
by Don Warrick

**Prayer: Beholding God's Glory**